JUDITH VON HALLE, born in Berlin in 1972, attended school in Germany and the USA and subsequently studied architecture, graduating in 1998. She first encountered anthroposophy in 1997, and began working as a member of staff at Rudolf Steiner House in Berlin, where she also lectured from 2001. In addition she had her own architectural practice. In 2004 she received the stigmata, which transformed her life. Her first book was published in German in 2005, and she now works principally as a lecturer and author. She lives in Berlin with her husband.

THE LORD'S PRAYER

By the same author:

And If He Has Not Been Raised ..., The Stations of Christ's Path to Spirit Man

THE LORD'S PRAYER

The Living Word of God

Judith von Halle

TEMPLE LODGE

Translated by Matthew Barton

Temple Lodge Publishing
Hillside House, The Square
Forest Row, RH18 5ES

www.templelodge.com

Published by Temple Lodge 2007

Originally published in German under the title *Das Vaterunser, Das gesprochene Wort Gottes* by Verlag am Goetheanum, Dornach, 2006

© Verlag am Goetheanum, Dornach 2006
This translation © Temple Lodge Publishing 2007

The author asserts her moral right to be identified as the author of this work

All rights reserved. No part of this publication may be reproduced, stored in a retrieval system, or transmitted, in any form or by any means, electronic, mechanical, photocopying or otherwise, without the prior permission of the publishers

A catalogue record for this book is available from the British Library

ISBN 978 1902636 85 6

Cover by Andrew Morgan Design featuring a mosaic from Ravenna, 'Christ and the Apostles at the Mount of Olives'
Typeset by DP Photosetting, Neath, West Glamorgan
Printed and bound by Cromwell Press Limited, Trowbridge, Wiltshire

Contents

Foreword   3

THE LORD'S PRAYER   15

Historical Circumstances at the Time of Christ   16

Preparation for Receiving the Prayer   24

The Gateway to the World of Spirit Was Opened   28

The Spoken Word of God   32

The Prayer as Mediator Between Worlds   36

The Word as Living Reality   45

The Words of the Doxology in the Lord's Prayer   49

The Lord's Prayer and the Sephiroth Tree   53

Emergence of the Trinity   58

The Path of Knowledge Through the Trunk of the Sephiroth Tree   67

The Lord's Prayer Grows as Human Beings Evolve   73

Personal Concluding Remarks   77

Approaches to Understanding the Christ Event

Volume 1

Foreword

This foreword aims to give some answers to questions I am repeatedly asked when I give lectures, or take part in discussion seminars.*

An unprepared reader might, quite understandably, be taken aback by the mode and content of some passages in this volume, since it includes descriptions of historical and supersensible facts and events which are related as self-evident truths without any reference to substantiating sources.

In actual personal encounter one can gain an authentic impression of the speaker, but in the inevitable absence of open-hearted personal contact with my reader — which makes it far easier to create a mood of human trust and dialogue as the basis for clear communication — I will try to record what I have to say in writing. I have formulated the fol-

---

* These questions have been dealt with more fully in the foreword to the collection of lectures *And If He Has Not Been Raised...* (Temple Lodge Publishing 2007).

lowing explanations and answers very precisely, knowing that such clarity could be interpreted as lack of modesty. At the same time though — which is why I am willing to take this risk — such clarity alone makes it possible to give anything like a full answer to questions that people ask me.

The contents of this volume have arisen from my own spiritual experience, and do not represent any kind of hypothesis or speculation, except where I expressly say that I am unable to make any definitive statement about a particular event or set of circumstances.

However, not every description stems from the same source of experience and perception. My spiritual experience relates, on the one hand, to a direct — one could even say sensory — involvement in the historical events at the time of Christ. This experience, granted to me following a process beginning in 2004 in which I received the stigmata, can be pictured as a kind of 'travelling back in time', involving all the sensory impressions we can have during ordinary waking life, but now in relation to a particular epoch and location. Thus the experience is not based on so-called visions or pure clairvoyance, nor imaginative pictures, but rather on direct witnessing of what actually happened on earth. Beside visual perceptions of the individuals participating in the events at the time of Christ, together with their surroundings, culture and way of life, all other senses available to us in normal waking consciousness are also involved. For instance the language being spoken can be heard, the ground beneath one's feet is felt, as are cold or heat.

The other source for the content presented here is quite different, yet no less authentic. It will be clear where accounts of the historical events pass over into a spiritual-scientific mode of observation.* This may well appear more neutral and sober than descriptions of sensory experience at the time of Christ. This is no doubt right and proper from a certain perspective, since it involves as precise a

---

* The term spiritual science refers to an investigation of spiritual realities which applies objective rigour of the kind only otherwise found in modern science. (This and all following footnotes have been added to the English edition by the translator or editor.)

'translation' as possible of what is present and perceptible in the world of spirit. We can access intuitions of these cosmic facts when our ego or 'I', on passing beyond the threshold, separates entirely from the astral sphere so that we — or in other words our 'I' — enters the realm of objectivity. Everyone has impressions of this kind during sleep, yet we rarely succeed in carrying these back into waking consciousness. It is a difficult task and therefore one which involves great responsibility, to transform these objective facts which our 'I' has absorbed beyond the threshold into real knowledge that is as truthful as is ordinary sense perception on its own, self-apparent terms. We need to check repeatedly whether our spiritual perception truly corresponds to the conceptual framework to which we assign it. Only when all results stand up in the face of such scrutiny should the pupil of spiritual science feel entitled to pass on his findings as spiritual knowledge.

Many people have spiritual perceptions nowadays (one often hears that this faculty is on the increase) — for instance on the etheric or astral plane.* These perceptions remain useless however, or can often even trigger grave confusion, if their real nature and context remains hidden to those who have them. For instance, someone may have perceptions of the etheric world, immersing himself in the sphere of elemental nature beings.† Yet statements about the elemental kingdom can only stand up to scrutiny, can only be truly objective, when we resurface again from that plane: in other words, when we do not solely immerse ourselves in the elemental beings' plane of experience but as it were raise it one level higher: to a perspective and point of observation from which we not only

---

* In Rudolf Steiner's view (see note on page 9), and that of the author, we possess, apart from our mineralized physical body, an etheric or life body which we share with the plant kingdom, and an astral or soul body which we have in common with animals. The etheric body is chiefly associated with rhythms, circulation and habitual ways of doing things, while the astral body is the seat of passions, emotions and soul. The fourth, and eternal, aspect of our being is the 'I' or ego which continues to exist after death and subsequently seeks reincarnation in a new body.

† Elemental beings are living but non-physical entities living in the various kingdoms of nature, of which human beings used to have more awareness. We find reference to them in folk-tales and literature as nature spirits (such as fire and water spirits).

can report on the nature of the elemental word, but can also have knowledge *about* this world. It is like swimming in a great expanse of water, an experience which enables us to say that the water is deep and cold. But only when we emerge into the air again like a bird can we judge whether this stretch of water is actually a large lake or possibly an ocean; and whether and where the water is surrounded by land or not, and which continent it is on. So before we can authentically integrate our perceptions into a wider, overall context, they always need to be examined from a higher standpoint.

It is spiritual science's achievement that we are nowadays able to transform our perceptions, through clear, trained thinking, into knowledge that is faithful to truth and reality.

The statements in this volume which do not contain sensory-based perceptions of events at the time of Christ derive from the source of knowledge just referred to. They are expressed cautiously, and with an appropriate sense of earnestness, and are in no way speculative interpretations. For this reason they may strike the reader as more factual or impersonal than the other accounts. This is due to the above-mentioned supra-personal level of objectivity beyond the threshold. Despite this they are my own authentic spiritual findings; and where, in contrast, they represent the findings of Rudolf Steiner,* this is expressly stated.

This second type of spiritual perception is not in any way a consequence of stigmatization, since it was present before this occurred. Since then, though, it has intensified.

After my lectures were published in book form,† some people asked me to give a precise exposition of my supposed path of schooling. I fully understand what underlies this desire, but apart from the fact that it was not my aim to address such issues in this book — since I do not wish to make

---

* 1861–1924. Rudolf Steiner founded the art and science of anthroposophy, a discipline that incorporates methods of personal development and philosophical and spiritual investigation, as well as fresh approaches to practical activities in fields such as medicine, agriculture, education and architecture.

† See note on p. 3. These lectures preceded publication of the present volume in the German language.

my own destiny the main subject of my deliberations, but instead to use the resources available to render the Christ event more comprehensible — such a 'development manual' would be very short and probably not at all of the kind that people wish or imagine. The mode of perception described above was already present in my early years, doubtless as a consequence of previous lives, and did not necessitate me pursuing, in this life, the arduous path of a hermit with all kinds of mortifications of the flesh and renunciations before my spiritual eyes were opened. Nor did it exclude, however, a certain discipline in my life as consequence of self-evident engagement with spiritual realities. My discipline or spiritual reverence in this life can be seen as a consequence of preparation. Nevertheless, 'continuity of awareness' beyond the threshold is always only possible when, with the greatest engagement and commitment, one has absorbed and continues to absorb the Christ event; when, in a way that is devoted, loving, humble and grateful, one turns not only one's heart and soul but also one's powers of enquiry to the world of spirit — until one feels so strongly moved by that greatest of all events in humanity's evolution that one starts to feel a tangible sense of the stigmata. Then one can have the profound experience that the great sacrifice of the Redeemer was also accomplished for each one of us, for our own humble being — within which, however, lies the seed of the divine.

Thus my potential to live consciously into the spiritual cosmos — also described as continuity of awareness — was already present before stigmatization occurred. When I also started experiencing the historical events at first hand, rather than this remaining pure experience I was able to bring together my capacity for supersensible knowledge with the historical events I witnessed. You could say that the tool was already present before the material it was to work upon. If you want to construct a violin you need a good tool, ready to hand before you begin — rather than starting to make one at the same time as the instrument you're making. Without a tool you may have the finest wood as raw material, but you will be unable to make a violin with it. In the present case, supersensible power of knowledge can provide the necessary tool for investigating the spiritual background to sensory processes and historical events.

Berlin, March 2006 *Judith von Halle*

Our Father

Which Art in the Heavens

Hallowed be thy Name

Thy Kingdom Come

Thy Will be Done

On Earth as it is in the Heavens

Give us this Day our Daily Bread

And Forgive us our Trespasses

As we Forgive them that Trespass Against us

Lead us not into Temptation

But Deliver us from Evil

A great deal has already been written on the theme with which this book is concerned. My aim in this volume is not to question the findings already available in the work of other spiritual researchers, let alone refute them. I only emphasize this because I suspect that little in this book will resonate with what you can read elsewhere about the Lord's Prayer. Instead, based on direct spiritual experience that involved my whole devotion and attention, this presentation on Christianity's oldest prayer arose very spontaneously in a way that enables me to share the experience with others. The starting point for this spiritual experience was hearing the original version of the Lord's Prayer from the lips of Jesus Christ. This experience kindled not only a witnessing of the actual historical events of the time, but above all the deeper spiritual perceptions which underpin this volume.

Historical Circumstances at the Time of Christ

Both in its origin and effect the Lord's Prayer is a unique, incomparable prayer which did not arise from a thought, a feeling or as consequence of a state of initiation. It is the only prayer humanity possesses which came directly from the mouth of the human being in whom a God resided. This prayer was spoken by the Logos itself. It is the spoken word of God, which, through the fact of the incarnation of this God in a human body, could penetrate directly through people's physical ears into their hearts at the turning point of time.*

As I experience it, the Redeemer spoke this original or archetypal prayer (at least) twice, in two different contexts and places, and to different people. On one occasion He spoke it to a larger gathering of His disciples among whom were present — as I remember it — the twelve disciples of the Last Supper. This did not take place in Jerusalem or in its immediate surroundings, but, judging by

---

* 'The turning point of time' is a phrase used by Rudolf Steiner of Christ's crucifixion and resurrection.

the landscape, in Galilee. On the second occasion He spoke the prayer for the group of women described below, during the night between Maundy Thursday and Good Friday. Here there were five of His intimate companions and pupils: the mother of Jesus; Mary Magdalene; the daughter of the mother's eldest sister, called Mariam Cleophas, whose son was Jacob the Younger; a sister of the mother, Mariam Salome, whose sons were Jacob the Elder and Little John (Zebedee); and also the mother of another disciple named Jochannan, later called Mark.

Although Christ had instructed the disciples that after His departure they should teach the prayer to people — and thus of course to the women who had a profound connection with Him — he knew that the men would find it difficult to overcome their traditional social views of women. To understand this one has to translate oneself back into a quite different time where certain laws, traditions and conventions prevailed. These arose from accepted religious customs and were very far removed from our own modern views of social community. It would never have occurred to people living in Palestine at the time of Christ to try to change the social and religious conditions of the time through a moral impulse of renewal. In the way that we nowadays enjoy the achievements of a certain social renewal, this was something which the Christ alone could bring about.

Various ideas suggested by historians or novelists, who believe they can trace the historical context of Jesus of Nazareth, arise from a moral template and social circumstances rooted in the 20th or 21st centuries. If we wish to penetrate the actual conditions prevailing 2000 years ago, this set of standards cannot serve as the basis for research. Serious research into Christ's times requires us to do something well-nigh impossible: distance ourselves from all moral and ethical contexts in which we stand today, and which all derive from western, Christian cultural evolution. Even if people dismiss the Christ mystery today, they are still deeply rooted in the impulse of freedom initiated by Christian culture and thought. All development since the time of Christ has been influenced by the Christ event — not least the development of the consciousness soul,* which itself enables us to adopt a critical stance towards the mystery of Golgotha.

I therefore wish to spend a moment trying to correct the distorted impressions made by colour magazines and novels (some of which are now best-sellers flooding the market) supposedly based on new discoveries or so-called 'historical research results'. The relationship of Jesus Christ to women was a special one, but did *not* have the implication clearly being attached to it at present. Instead it had a quite different foundation. At the time of Christ it was unimaginable for a Jewish woman to approach the spiritual teacher too intimately. We can therefore call it a radical innovation that an initiate of that time devoted efforts to the spiritual instruction of women. In this context Mary Magdalene, as individual, is repeatedly brought into disrepute today. But

---

* The consciousness soul is a state of objective, onlooker consciousness and mature responsibility, one perhaps typified at present by swiftly developing awareness of the need to care for the planet.

these claims are wholly inaccurate, for such conduct simply does not correspond to the way people related to each other in those times. Spiritual instruction of women showed, rather, that it was not spiritual initiation of men or women that was involved, but that of *human* souls, who were accorded such great significance that they could bear the responsibility of spreading Christianity throughout the world. Thus such theories, or one might say tasteless fantasies as are prevalent today, which are quite alien to the true spirit of those times, show merely a lack of capacity to properly assess the nature of a relationship such as that between Mary Magdalene and the Christ being. Mary Magdalene gave Christ her most devoted sympathy and the purest, most innocent love – a stance of soul which we may perhaps partly rediscover in the feeling we can have towards a child: a willingness to do everything for him, including unhesitatingly sacrificing our life. In supposedly 'progressive' descriptions no account at all is taken of the nature of the encounter of a soul with the Son of God in human form, let alone its great significance. Here we see the abysmal trend of our age, the anti-Zeitgeist, which dissipates the whole spiritual context of events at the turning point of time, rendering it a tissue of rumour and illusion, and making Christ's initiates into figures in a modern farce.

Let me repeat: the fact that Christ also instructed women in teachings about the kingdom that is not of *this* world, shows how little account the representative of humanity took, in our time's materialistic and sensory terms, of men and women as mere representatives of the sexes. It was this very distinction, as primary criterion, that Jesus Christ repeatedly tried to soften in the hearts and minds of the people of those times. We can discover that Christ was indeed a 'rule-breaker'. He repeatedly and intentionally violated rules not imbued with a living, valid purpose. Christ healed almost without exception on Sabbath days, in the clear knowledge that any kind of work not directly seen as homage to God was prohibited on that day. In this way he tried to give humanity a new, self-directed understanding of the significance of homage to God — for instance to those who rushed past starving beggars in their haste to make their offerings of bread in the temple, as required by the law. What does someone do with a left-over loaf of bread? Does he place it in the temple fire as an offering of thanks to God, who makes the corn grow so that bread can be made; or does he give it to the hungry and thus protect God's creature from death? Today we would have little difficulty in deciding, but for people at the time of Christ this idea was revolutionary. The degree to which people at the turning point of time were rooted in this moral code is, ultimately, demonstrated by the sentencing to death of Jesus Christ: it can be argued that this was due to his infringement of the Sabbath law.

Thus, through the deeds of Jesus Christ in various spheres of life, the old laws were re-formed into new possibilities of approaching God; yet people found it difficult to participate in this transformation — for instance the men in relation to the women whom Christ taught. Repeatedly, therefore, there was conflict between the disciples and their master who, in their view, associated too freely, generously and unconventionally with women. This conduct by the disciples may have been one reason why Christ also spoke the Lord's Prayer to women shortly before His death.

After the Last Supper and shortly before He climbed the Mount of Olives with the men, He withdrew with the women to an ancient sacred place at the foot of the Mount — close to the river Cidron in the South — where King David had once touched the earth with his hands in a vague yet presageful foreshadowing of the fact that the Redeemer would tarry here for a while before his last journey.

It was here that Christ gave the Lord's Prayer to the women. On Mary Magdalene, in particular, the prayer left a mighty impression — the latter word signifying here something literal: it was inscribed into her soul. In relation to his spiritual study of the bodily sheaths* and the development of new spirit organs, Rudolf Steiner speaks at various times of an 'impress' which, in sleep and through death, forms and informs each respective sheath in a subsequent life. The Lord's Prayer engraved itself indelibly into

---

* These 'sheaths' are the physical, etheric and astral bodies referred to earlier, into which the 'I' incarnates.

those who heard it from Jesus Christ's own mouth, and were fortunate enough to absorb it.

Preparation for Receiving the Prayer

Before Christ gave the Lord's Prayer to the disciples and the women, he turned to them in the warmest and most loving way, spoke to them and invigorated them with His perfected, unfathomable wisdom and goodness. It was a soul impression such as one can have in the image of Christ the Son of God who holds the golden stars in His hand, as described in the words of the Apocalypse of St John: the Christ sun, surrounded by His pupils as stars, whom He prepares in a unique way for the opening door to the world of spirit. It was a picture of purity, resting in majestic beauty, a moment of eternity beyond all temporal things.

In order to represent the way in which the Redeemer prepared His closest and dearest disciples to receive the Lord's Prayer — for this was not mere communication but a means by which they experienced the workings of the world of spirit through speech, and the preparation for this was, accordingly, very significant — I would like to try to translate what He spoke to them beforehand. I cannot say with any certainty whether this 'speech' was in Aramaic or even in earthly words at all, or whether he laid it directly into their receptive souls. I will attempt to reproduce the inner content of the preparation granted to His disciples:

> *All of you together are like the heavenly*
>   *constellations.*
> *You represent what is imperishable in the world,*
>   *and in the future. This you bear within you.*
> *Just as the stars encircle and transmute the world,*
>   *so you too will encircle and transmute the world,*
> *and the gaze of human beings will turn to you as to*
>   *the stars.*
> *You will be to them as the stars, because I ray out*
>   *within you, and they will be illumined through*
>   *you.*

In this way He prepared them to receive the prayer which has continued to accompany humanity to this day, and will do so into the far-distant future.

As Christ spoke the Lord's Prayer to the disciples and women, the consciousness soul of those present was addressed for the first time, and each individual 'I' was touched.

Before and above all after He had given them the Lord's Prayer, He spoke with them, and it seemed to them as though He addressed all of them together and yet each one individually.

Each disciple, each pupil had the sense that the world's saviour was now addressing his eternal, unique, individual being, which is neither male nor female. Each one had the sense that Christ had placed the spoken prayer into his soul, and said: *Speak it, Shimon!, Speak it, Joche!, Speak it, Jaakov!, Speak it, Mariam! ...*

After they had absorbed the prayer into their hearts, their experiences appeared to them with a certainty which He himself chased into them like a roaring storm. What they had experienced, felt and seen through the Lord's Prayer was so mighty that they were unable to keep it all living in their awareness. In general we do not tend to have a precise recall of our perceptions, so that over time our memory of what we have experienced is diluted or even starts to change to match our own ideas of it. For this reason He said to them:

> *Do not bear witness to what your eyes have seen. Bear witness that what you have seen with your own eyes is the truth.*

The gift of the Lord's Prayer involved a prefiguring of what could only arise irrevocably as 'I' impulse after or through the resurrection. It was similar with the Last Supper which was celebrated as transformation of bread and wine even before the earth had become the body of Christ. By descending to earth and incarnating in a human body, Christ himself could inaugurate the mysteries of the New Testament, which during his lifetime were like a foreshadowing or advance enactment of the actual mysteries to come. The same was true of what Christ's disciples and pupils received with the Lord's Prayer. The Lord's Prayer was given them by a God, but because He had entered a mortal human frame, it was given them in a direct sense, from one person to another, from mouth to ear. Concealed in this act — as the basis for all future human knowledge — lies the historical fact in human evolution of the actual incarnation of the Logos. It was not through a parable, not through a legend as moral instruction, but solely through the physical presence of a God on earth that these mysteries of the New Testament could be given directly to human beings at the turning point of time; and only by this means was this prayer preserved unchanged throughout millennia: through the unique confluence of a divine being with a mortal human entity.

THE GATEWAY TO THE WORLD OF SPIRIT WAS OPENED

As Christ spoke the mystery words of this prayer to His disciples, as His words were engraved in them, they were also raised up from the earth for a brief moment. This levitation had a special significance in the three years* of Christ's life on earth. It occurred

---

* The 'three years' refers to the period of Christ's incarnation in the body of Jesus.

because Christ was not yet able to work wholly from within the human being outwards, as He can today, because He had not yet created this possibility by passing through death and resurrection. The disciples did not pass through an initiation or temple sleep in the old sense, but what occurred can be called an initiation, one lying in an intermediary stage between the old and the new path. They could only experience all this in a condition that was slightly released from the earth. The three disciples Simon Peter, Jacob and John experienced a similar initiation state at the Transfiguration on the Mount.

This impression on their souls was so mighty that, when the last word had resounded and the great imaginations, inspirations and intuitions that had streamed into them through the essence and tone of the words had faded, they sank down and forgot all the mystery wisdoms vouchsafed to them in a great spiritual vision. This supposed weakness should not however be viewed as such. We need to try to put ourselves in the place of someone before whom the being of the primal Creator appears — visible, tangible, audible, as a supersensible love and radiant wisdom too great to grasp, pouring into the soul. People have little idea how powerful the impressions and revelations were that were granted to the disciples through utterance of the Lord's Prayer by the mouth of God. The gateway to the world of spirit was opened, and the Guardian of the Threshold was Christ Himself. He enabled them to pass the threshold so that their souls could be penetrated by the great cosmic wisdoms. The disciples were overwhelmed by this, not yet knowing the 'I' experience and conscious forces of our own times, but living at a period in which the human gaze had been darkened for perception of the worlds of spirit. We have to realize that the so-called twelve disciples, in particular, were not initiates of the pre-Christian mysteries. It was necessary for these disciples to have no share in the old forms of initiation which, at the time of Jesus Christ, had fallen into degeneracy: in this way the earthly presence of the God could be accepted and absorbed by them in a much less hampered way. They had not been trained in the old capacity of reading the occult script, and so they initially forgot the visions they had seen in their state of spiritual elevation. They *had* to forget the content of the old mysteries, because freedom is a gift of Christ. The freedom to regain occult knowledge, through forces of consciousness one develops oneself rather than receiving it as wisdom from above, was a gift of Christ, and one they were allowed to take advantage of.

While they did not forget the words of the Lord's Prayer, they did forget the wisdom that lives in it. However, the profound shock remained with them, and an awareness that they had experienced something that was more real than anything else, and that they now needed to strive for this through great spans of time, through work and effort, in devotion and love.

This certainty had imbued them, and rendered them strong for their further path after Jesus Christ had continued on His way. He remained as exemplar of the archetypal Christian, and this gave them the impetus to dedicate their lives to the Christ. They had become witnesses to the reality of the spirit, something recalled in the significance of the word 'martyrion', which means 'witness'.

The Spoken Word of God

And now I would like to draw your attention to something particular:

The words of the Lord's Prayer, unlike all other cult and ritual words of those times, were *not sung but spoken*.

In the old rites it was law and tradition that any word directed to God should rise from the earth to the heavens via a sacred 'circuit' which consisted of a chanted singsong.

In the ancient Hebraic rites, prayers were never allowed to be spoken, but had to be sung in accordance with a strictly prescribed series of tones. The melody was like the smoke of a burnt offering, which rose up into higher worlds. These strictly specified melodies lifted people from the body into another sphere. The 'I' was dulled, and a group-soul condition was the bearer of the rites of worship. This precisely prescribed singsong induced a trance-like state in worshippers.

Christ, the Word become flesh, directed the disciples to *speak* to the Father. The spoken word has the strongest effect on the 'I'. To make this clear we can consider for a moment the phenomenon of stuttering, particularly in children, which can be attributed to a passing weakening of the 'I' — for instance through the arrival of a new sibling who deprives an older child of the mother's undivided attention. The barely awoken child 'I' cannot cope with directly spoken words. Stuttering improves if the child does not speak the phrases he wants to say, but produces them in a singsong intonation, until his inmost core has been strengthened again. The appearance of Christ, one can say, produced such a strengthening, as the beginning of words spoken with full awareness. It is surely a part of every person's path of self-development to learn not to spout indiscriminately every thought that comes into our heads, but to handle our words with ever greater reflection and care. Today we need to relearn the art of speaking with spiritual responsibility. Over time people will increasingly recognize the significance of the Word, learning to direct speech with their will so that they can use it to give real impetus, to shape or also unshape things — depending on whether the Word is used for good or ill, for human benefit or to sow discord. In future the human being will grow powerful in a new way by directing the Word towards his human and natural surroundings.

Through spoken utterance alone the words of the Lord's Prayer entered the disciples' consciousness soul. The Logos in its true destiny appeared amongst the disciples: the Word became flesh. This made their 'I' dynamically active in a way that had never previously occurred. After Jesus had departed they themselves had to speak the magic formulations in a self-directed, autonomous way. Before the death and resurrection of Jesus Christ they did not speak these words themselves, but He alone spoke them. And they experienced the effect that the prayer could have through the mouth of God — in other words they had a foreshadowing vision of what would resound from their own mouths in the most distant future. Christ gave them this vision to spur them on and guide them. Only after Whitsun did they speak the prayer themselves. In every word they spoke, disrobed from the protective veil of appearance, or maya, they were permeated with the living spirit of the Trinity. Everything that ever was or would be, lived and issued from their words. They found themselves embedded in an unknown reality — particularly at the moment when they heard the living beings of the Word for the first time, directly from the mouth of the Redeemer. The words, derived from their own mother tongue, appeared to them initially as shockingly hard, severe and powerful, and in their direct finality almost obdurate and remorseless.

By tying in prayers indirectly addressed to Jahve via the sun to strictly prescribed singsong chant sequences, the priests had for many centuries avoided the direct effect of divine reality's influx into human beings in songless speech. They knew that the human being was not yet ready for the directly spoken word, and that this could be made possible only by the Word become flesh, the Christ.

Anyone who tries singing the Lord's Prayer — as is sometimes done in the Catholic Church — will find himself being drawn back into a former time, before the time when Christ's gift of the Lord's Prayer was to overcome dilution of the power of the Word caused by ritual chanting.

The Prayer as Mediator Between Worlds

I now want to give a glimpse of the spiritual experience this prayer gives rise to: what the pupil of spiritual science who awakens beyond the threshold can experience nowadays, and what the disciples and women also perceived at the turning point of time in a 'pre-conscious' condition through the presence of Christ.

The Lord's Prayer resounds of course in the physical, earthly world. But it resounds also beyond the threshold. It is a kind of mediator between these two worlds and joins them together. Of course these two worlds are always joined, so that we can only speak of a mediating activity that joins these worlds from the perspective of our current state of human consciousness. To the seer's gaze, speaking the Lord's Prayer unites two worlds which otherwise stand distinct from one another in ordinary perception, so that one world – the spiritual – usually remains invisible. If the human being can direct his gaze to these two worlds, he gains insight into the way they interact, and the manifestations arising from them. Then he perceives that every sensory perception on this side of the threshold has a primal source, has its true existence beyond the threshold. What we see here in the physical sense-world as the colour of a rose, is an expression of what the rose is beyond the threshold. This also holds true for the spoken word, and for the concepts and numbers which are linked with individual letters in Hebrew and Aramaic. Those who heard the Lord's Prayer from the mouth of Christ thus experienced the living, true being of words. This living, true being of the Word had been concealed from them previously. What they experienced through words in the sensory world approached the nature of the Word only as a kind of reflection. A reflection, it is true, is a likeness of a being, but is never that being itself. But now the truth of the Lord's Prayer beyond the threshold became a direct experience for them, and this process led them to insight into great cosmic mysteries.

The reality of words stood before them in images,

colours, sounds, yet not in the way we generally perceive images, colours and tones through our sensory organs; instead they experienced the essence of a colour, the essence of a sound, smell or taste, and were thus able to experience the cosmic laws underlying sensory phenomena. They saw the magnificent harmony connecting all the apparently disconnected, chance phenomena of the sensory world; they saw the most intricate and yet at the same time simple and perfect whole integrating everything with everything else; they saw that everything is embedded in a divine order, in which the human being and the spiritual hierarchies also have their place. And they experienced this order and harmony through the central, shaping and mediating power of the Christ being.

Anyone who speaks the Lord's Prayer today encounters something similar to those who first heard and prayed it. It is really always the same living quality we encounter when we pray it. But there are many different developmental stages on a path of incarnation, so we experience this prayer in different ways: in the past with greater power of feeling, and in the future with ever greater clarity of knowledge. We should just ponder for a moment how often in the past 2000 years we have spoken this prayer in different incarnations! It has assumed a different significance in each context, and this will continue to be true into the furthest future.

Christ awoke the words to life. Spoken by Him, living spirit beings were born in the earth's ether, resounding to the disciples' senses. Previously these had lived as purely spiritual truths beyond the threshold. Each word, each sound leads an independent existence in the form of a cosmic mystery. The whole cosmos is contained in every word. Yet, as the disciples experienced this, each single word also released itself from the cosmos despite continuing to bear it and preserve it within itself. Every word stood for itself alone as a unique and sense-encompassed cosmic wisdom. As wondrous, divine life, each one inhabited its own cosmos. These different, living creations pulsed together in harmony: fifty different wisdom-filled worlds offering a simple and at the same time unfathomably deep revelation of knowledge of the primal ground of the divine world and its connection with human evolution.

In Aramaic the original version of the Lord's Prayer contains fifty words as Christ gave them to the disciples and the women. In ancient Judaic esotericism, the number 50 was not only already the very essence of redemption but also stood for the culmination of 49, of 7 × 7, which was seen as the stages of incarnation through earth evolution.

Once we have passed through these phases of 7 × 7 — let us also put it in anthroposophical terms:* once we have passed through seven cultural epochs times seven great epochs — we have completed our earthly pilgrimage and stand before the perfection of our path. Beyond 49 we enter the realm of 50, that of revelation, and this will signify the origin of a new planetary condition.†

---

* Anthroposophy was the name Rudolf Steiner gave to his wide-ranging Christ-centred philosophy and practice. Literally it means 'wisdom of the human being'.

† This refers to the evolutionary stages through which the human being has passed and will pass in future. Once we have completed our evolution on earth through different 'cultural epochs', the essence of all that human beings have developed here will pass into a new state or planetary embodiment. Thus one can see the planet itself in similar terms to each individual: just as we reincarnate into a new body and set of conditions, so eventually will the whole planet.

With every spoken word the disciples encountered a new, resonant wisdom: they grew and flourished like a plant in spring that sprouts from a seed concealed in the earth. Yet though these insights entered them as swiftly as the words resounded, they arose — in a way similar to the plant — from something concealed and hidden. As the plant grows from the seed lying hidden from view in the ground, what had previously been hidden to them grew, blossomed and flourished towards the world of spirit.

Thus these living beings lived, resounded and 'coloured' their way into the earthly world. This no longer occurred through the old initiation sleep lasting several days, during which pupils had to leave the body in order to have spiritual perceptions, but the disciples were able to have these perceptions in their earthly body.

The experience granted to them through the utterance of words by the Word become flesh, was of undreamed light and clarity. Through Him they experienced what a human being will be able to bring forth at the end of earth evolution when he himself speaks these words. They had this experience solely through the mouth of Christ. At the end of earth evolution the human being will be able to produce these spiritual creations through his mouth. In the whole mantric verse, in the whole prayer, the cosmos was living in such a way that, poured into speech forms, it bore the reality of the Trinity down to earth.

Thus they — as we today — were initiation pupils. The disciples and women were so, however, through Christ's direct help. The initiation pupil prefigures what people will be able to do in future. He is granted a supra-earthly perspective, and his soul becomes and perceives objectively:

The truths of the past	Father
The truths of the present	Son
The truths of the future	Holy Spirit

In this way the initiation pupil — and the disciples and women of that time — are vouchsafed that supersensible perspective which unites past, present and future. When all three streams of time flow together in the human being's inner observation and insight, uniting in his awareness, then he has emerged from the passage of time, and the earth soul becomes cosmic soul.

The whole panorama of living cosmic realities was uniquely embodied for the disciples' earthly and supra-earthly organs of perception by the Christ Himself. After the mystery revelations of the spirit Word, he then spoke to their souls thus:

> *My human brothers, speak these words until they*
>   *once again receive their vitality through you!*
> *When, a long time hence, they live in you, through*
>   *you, as they now do through me, then the*
>   *kingdom of the Father will come to you, and you*
>   *to it.*
> *Live with these words, make yourself ready*
>   *through them*
> *to dispel their magic power*
> *through the force of your spirit knowledge!*

The human being thus has to speak these magical words until they transform him by his own powers; until, by having penetrated the Christ being in himself, he can eventually enliven them as Christ did at the turning point of time. 'Magic' always indicates an effect whose cause one cannot consciously fathom. This commentary and further explanation by Christ gave the disciples an inkling that they must demystify the prayer themselves, through their own developing awareness. Also, that this was a task that must be carried on through the future until the earth has been spiritualized.

But one other precondition for this spiritualization was necessary: such a condition can only be achieved through the new mysteries, and specifically a new covenant with humanity. We find an indication of this new covenant in the Lord's Prayer, in the plural form that runs through all the petitions in the prayer. The Lord's Prayer counteracts egotistic impulses by petitioning as a community of spirit. It could be objected that the plural form was already present in the pre-Christian Jewish rite, as is indeed the case. Yet its petitions were strictly embedded in a folk covenant with a particular race. Now, instead, our appeal arises from a universally human community. The new covenant only arises where a whole range of different human beings individually address the world of spirit, yet do so in the light of a common spiritual striving.

The Word as Living Reality

We have already referred to the vibrant vitality of the words of the Lord's Prayer. I would now like to give a brief outline of the nature and content of these spiritual realities.

On one occasion Rudolf Steiner described how other magic formulae worked on human beings both shortly before and during the time of Christ. Here we must give two different meanings to the term 'magic'. Witness of the historical events confirms that priests used certain speech-images to create effects that appeared to emanate from a living word. The process worked by tying letters to a concept; the reader or listener did not really perceive the letters as such, nor the spiritual realities underlying them, but an image that he linked to the letters. This image was only living to the extent that an image can be. In fact it was static and fixed, only supposedly enlivened, at most, through ideas and concepts. When someone living at the time of Christ saw or heard the letter ב (Beht), the association 'house' arose in him. It is true that the letter B rightly stands for the concept 'house' (as is clear from eurythmy), yet the letter is deprived of the vitality of its true being if, at the same time, the fixed concept of a certain type of building made of stone and mortar is linked with it. The priests mediated to people a perception of spiritual worlds and wisdom, and the reflection of the essence of words rather than their actual, vital being — which cannot be mediated through a priest as representative, but must be experienced directly by each individual. Thus the priests spoke the old formulae which were magical in a different sense, by working through associations that required images to give the words impact and effect.

The Lord's Prayer however gives rise to the opposite path in the inward experience of someone who prays: the words embody living realities, and not merely their reflected concept.

This living penetration led in the disciples to something that all initiates of post-Christian times experienced and experience. And when someone who undergoes this experience consciously tries to reveal it to his fellows, he coins a corresponding

THE WORD AS LIVING REALITY

image of truth — translated into concepts and symbols — whose being becomes manifest to his spirit-expanded soul. One can also speak of spiritual laws that clothe themselves in a true image. Thus for the disciples and women, the temple's great object of worship was revealed, the cast-metal symbol of which appeared to their spiritual vision. They received knowledge of the true nature of the wisdom expressed in the seven-branched candelabrum. And the following wisdoms were linked with this true image:

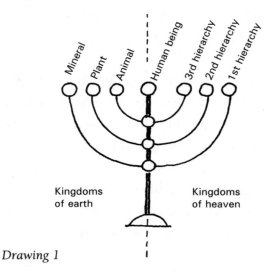

Drawing 1

What can be described as the unfalsified gnosis is, after all, knowledge of spiritual worlds that extends far back into the pre-Christian past of humanity's evolution. This knowledge streamed down into human beings from above. They experienced the world of spirit in a dreamlike picture consciousness. Nothing about this ancient gnosis is untrue, but since the time of Christ it is an outmoded path because the direction of the stream has reversed. Christ leads human beings back to a conscious rediscovery of gnostic truths. Through the Word we fathom the essence of the image.

From below upwards the disciples came autonomously to knowledge of the tree. They perceived themselves in this living image of truth, recognizing where we stand as humanity — that is, at the boundary between a being of earth and a divine being (see *Drawing 1*: central axis), and that in the human being the Trinity directly unites the realms to the right and left of the central axis. (See *Drawing 1*: the links running through the central axis, joining the three kingdoms of earth with the three supersensible kingdoms. The three paths between the node points correspond to the Trinity.)

The Words of the Doxology in the Lord's Prayer

In order to sanctify this sense of insight and knowledge, and to preserve it for subsequent generations, the first Christians added something to the Lord's Prayer which can only mature as knowledge in human beings through praying the *Our Father* — that is, an awareness of the threefold reality of the human being. They expressed this in the words:

> *For Thine is the kingdom, the power and the glory, for ever and ever.*

The human being who awakens to spiritual consciousness passes inwardly through these realities: kingdom — power — glory — eternity (see *Drawing 1*: proceeding from below upwards through the four node points on the central axis). They added this to the prayer as a result of their own, autonomous experience that arose through speaking the prayer. This could only ripen through praying the *Our Father*. Because they had their own, independent 'candelabrum experience', they were able to connect this so-called doxology, as confirmation of the insight they had gained, directly to the prayer they had so fully penetrated.

Out of this experience, which takes form as the true image of the seven-branched candelabrum, the Menorah, a still more comprehensive insight grew and developed, which is reflected in the living truth of the image of another tree.

While one could say that the 'candelabrum experience' had revealed the tree of cosmic realms to them, now a new tree stood before the disciples' spiritual eyes, which we can call the tree of the human being or of knowledge. It is, let me mention in passing, certainly not true to say that very clever people once 'came up' with the idea of this tree; but it actually comes to meet the initiation pupil as reality when he passes the door that leads beyond the veil of the senses. Through this tree created by the spoken words of the Lord's Prayer, the disciples experienced how their bodily sheaths were each, separately, addressed. Rudolf Steiner once* demonstrated this special state of affairs in a drawing which in a certain sense prepares the ground for this tree arising in the Lord's Prayer.

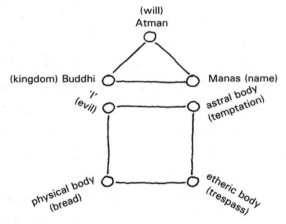

Drawing 2

The summit, or crown, of this tree is the will.

The will of God is not something that is imposed on human beings like the tablets of the Law on

---

* Lecture by R. Steiner given on 28 January 1907, in GA 96, *Ursprungsimpulse der Geistewissenschaft*, Dornach 1989. English version in *The Lord's Prayer*, Rudolf Steiner Press, Sussex 2007.

Mount Sinai. If we speak the Lord's Prayer over many incarnations, it dawns on us that our own conscious, I-guided will is the will of God — for we will discover that what can be designated as true and pure cosmic will can only ever be the *one* divine will. Thus, as we ask the world of spirit in these words of prayer for the divine will to work and hold sway on the earth — *thy will be done, as it is in the heavens, so also on the earth* — we experience an enlivening of our own 'I', which ultimately leads us to seek and recognize the divine will in ourselves. This mood gives rise to the exclamation: *Not my will but thine!* It seems to be a widespread misunderstanding that the 'I' is active in the human will, or that it produces the will. Yet the divine will in the human being has no ego or anything remotely selfish. As soon as we recognize the selflessness of the will it begins to exert a healing effect on us. The Lord's Prayer is a selfless prayer of peace. We can only speak the petitions of the Lord's Prayer in a wholly unegotistic way. In speaking the Lord's Prayer we are not just asking for our own wellbeing but for that of all humanity. First a feeling, and later conscious awareness is stimulated through the fact that we live by virtue of the deeds of the divine hierarchies, and that this is the only way in which we can live in the world. The Lord's Prayer is thus a peace prayer. It creates consciousness of the powers of temptation and rigidification. In consequence we can gain control over these powers, and the prayer becomes a life-bringing utterance.

The four lower or earthly bodily sheaths which constitute us are connected with the *petitions of the Lord's Prayer*. The three higher, divine-spiritual sheaths,* are connected with the *invocations*. However this is only a first part of the tree which Jewish tradition designates by the name *Sephiroth tree* (meaning 'number-tree', from 'sephira' = number).

The Lord's Prayer and the Sephiroth Tree

The Lord's Prayer is intimately linked with the Aramaic language, and thus also with the Hebrew

---

* These higher sheaths, whose development extends into the far future and will be achieved by transforming the lower sheaths of physical, etheric and astral bodies, are called: Spirit Self, Life Spirit and Atman.

letters. At the time of Christ the Aramaic language was the national or common language of the Jewish people in Palestine, while Hebrew — the language of the priests, used in religious worship — was barely spoken or understood. However the alphabet, and the symbols and the numbers associated with them, were identical in Hebrew and new Aramaic. We should not imagine that the language Christ spoke on earth was mere chance, or even insignificant. The fact that this incarnated God spoke Aramaic is as 'meaningless' as the fact that He incarnated into the context of the Jewish race and its customs.

The Word-become-flesh Himself spoke these sacred words in Aramaic. I have never heard the Christ speak to his disciples in Greek. To my perception He spoke the Lord's Prayer in Aramaic; and it was specifically these 22 letters of the Hebrew-Aramaic alphabet, so deeply familiar to the disciples, which formed the basis for gaining access to the spiritual revelations beyond the threshold which merged into these Aramaic words. We can therefore have the sense that this prayer should be spoken in people's common vernacular, in whatever language is most familiar to them. It should be spoken in all human languages, as we should access spiritual experience in prayer spoken in the language to whose spirit we are most intimately connected.

And thus the 22 letters of the Hebrew alphabet, forming the basis of their Aramaic mother tongue, stood before the disciples and the women as real beings of a previously hidden world. These 22 letters marked the branches of this growing and branching tree, the paths between the Sephiroth (the numbers). In turn the Sephiroth — emanations which formed the human being out of the divine primal unity — are the spiritual reality working in the earthly human being and the tangible, physical world. The Sephiroth (*Drawing 3*: 1–10, see p. 57) stood before the disciples like the leaves or blossoms sprouting from the branches of a tree, and they recognized that they themselves bore this tree with them, and that the nature of this tree represented their own true, human nature. Thus one can recognize that the tree does not arise from the letters and numbers, but the reverse is true: the 22 letters do not have merely chance correspondence with spiritual truths, nor have they been pressed into a devised schema, but at the dawn of time this wisdom was read from the world of spirit and formed into earthly numbers and letters. The letters first arose from the entity of the 'tree of knowledge', which is why we do not need the 22 letters of the Hebrew or Aramaic alphabet today in order to gain insight into the true nature of the words of the Lord's Prayer. The tree as spiritual reality stands beyond the threshold to the world of spirit, and each one of us — irrespective of our language and culture — can penetrate to vision of this tree. The name of this experiential insight and knowledge is spiritual science.

Yet the relationship between the language of that time and the tree of knowledge clearly shows how the wisdom streaming from the cosmos was once poured into the form of words. The prologue to the Gospel of St John states: *In the beginning was the Word* (see *Drawing 3*).

THE LORD'S PRAYER AND THE SEPHIROTH TREE

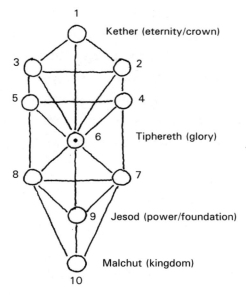

Drawing 3

(In this extended tree we can recognize the 'tree' in Rudolf Steiner's sketch, i.e. the square and the upper triangle.)

Like a stroke of lightning the disciples and the women could suddenly grasp the reality of reincarnation through the essence of this tree. They felt: *It is to this that my 'I' can arise. I bear this tree within me, but I have to work through it from below upwards with my own conscious forces so that it can blossom in the earthly world as vitally as in the other world. Yet no autonomous human 'I' is capable of attaining this goal immediately, but needs a long, long path of evolution to do so!* Through this act, for the first time, higher understanding was kindled in them of the need for individual responsibility as the basis for human evolution arising through karma.

Emergence of the Trinity

The disciples recognized Christ as the Son of God who had descended to earth — as the central power of the Trinity. In the tree of spirit this works through the sephira *Tiphereth*, the number 6 (see *Drawing 3*). *Tiphereth* can be translated — very imperfectly — as 'beauty', 'harmony' or 'glory'. *Tiphereth*, which is in fact the Messiah, stands at the midpoint of the tree, at the central balancing axis, the centre of the trunk. One can also say that the glory of the Son stands at the centre of the four earthly bodily sheaths, and that it alone first kindles the activity of the 'I', subsequently bringing the seed of the higher bodies (the upper triangle) into existence (see *Drawing 4*; also *Drawing 2*).

The central power of the Trinity, the Christ power, enables the earthly quadrilateral to be penetrated and opened. And through this same central power the disciples for the first time had a brief but overwhelming sense of the reality of the Trinity.

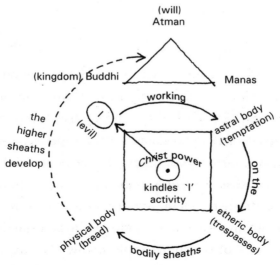

Drawing 4

In the Roman Catholic rite the formula for the transubstantiation in the Eucharist preserves a hint of what these original Christians felt and what we also rediscover, in a metamorphosed form, in the Rosicrucian verse. The priest says:

> *Through him,*
> *with him,*
> *and*
> *in him,*
> *in the unity of the Holy Spirit,*
> *all glory and honour is yours,*
>> [the words used once to be: 'power' and 'glory']
>
> *almighty Father,*
> *now and forever.*

The disciples experienced the Christ in the centre of their own being. From this point, issuing from the heart, they were able through the Christ mystery to experience the 'through', 'with' and 'in' Him (the Son) in union with the 'almighty Father' and the 'Holy Spirit'. Only through Christ, the middle member of the Trinity, through his physical presence among them, were they able to recognize the Trinity as he spoke the words of the Lord's Prayer. This living knowledge was new to the disciples, for they had never previously been able to form any conception of God's threefold nature.

This invocation of the Three-in-One comes to expression in the Catholic transubstantiation formula.

Now there is yet another vestige preserved in this formula from the times of those who first prayed the *Our Father*: this is where, in conclusion, it states

> [...]
> *all power and glory be yours*
> *now and forever.*

It is striking that at the place in the service which celebrates the highest gift of Christ, the transformation of his body, we have the same phrases that were added by the first Christians to the Lord's Prayer, as a kind of annex to the actual petitions. These original Christians knew how to speak the prayer in the right way, and to clothe their objective, soul-spiritual feelings in words:

For thine is the kingdom
the power and the glory
for ever and ever
[End of Lord's Prayer / 'doxology']

[...]
all power and glory be yours
now and forever. [Transubstantiation formula]

In the words of the Transubstantiation, the word 'now' refers to the 'kingdom' of the doxology which exists on earth through divine power — in other words the earthly kingdom as opposed to the heavenly kingdom of 'forever'.

At this very point in the Communion, the Transubstantiation, stand the words spoken by the first Christians at the end of the Lord's Prayer when they themselves had undergone a transformation through speech — a transformation into the human spirit.

This formula (kingdom, power, glory, forever) is something we also find in the true image of the seven-branched candelabrum, as well as in the Sephiroth tree, the tree of knowledge (see *Drawings 5* and *6*).

EMERGENCE OF THE TRINITY

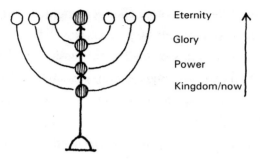

Drawing 5

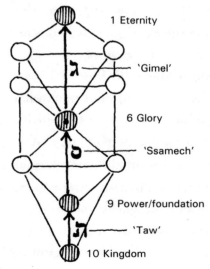

Drawing 6

People at the time of Christ were right to augment this archetypal prayer they had received from Christ. These additional words give expression to the personal response and engagement we can find through re-enlivening this mystery prayer: engagement arising through our independent knowledge of God.

People of the time experienced the Trinity through this spiritual tree, and recognized in its central axis (which Rudolf Steiner did not include in *Drawing 2* since he was only speaking of the words of Christ and not the appended doxology) the threefold Godhead of Father, Son and Holy Spirit working in the human being.

The path through 10, 9, 6 to 1 (see *Drawing 6*, dark-shaded Sephiroth) is the one which the human being develops. It is a path which we pursue through our own autonomy. Christ left it to his human brothers, through conscious self-elevation to the world of spirit, through praying the *Our Father*, to attain knowledge of this path.

> *For thine is the kingdom* (10), the *power* (9) and the *glory* (6), for *ever and ever* (1)

In the tree of knowledge the path through 10, 9, 6 to 1 is marked by the tree's actual trunk. Even if it might seem paradoxical, we can say that the tree trunk only starts to grow (from 10 towards 1) when we recognize that there is a trunk.

This tree of emanation, initially embodied in the symbol of the seven-branched candelabrum, is now no longer experienced from above downwards but instead, through Christ's descent to earth and the fact that we can now elevate ourselves through our own powers to knowledge of the world of spirit, from below upwards. In pre-Christian times initiates did indeed view the tree from the opposite perspective (from above downwards); and with this tree of emanation one can say that only the God-given, passive side of human nature was addressed, which was also why only sung words were directed to God. The seven-branched candelabrum is the 'right' way round, despite the fact that the sensory, cast-metal image of its spiritual essence was already created in pre-Christian times. Although people did not yet experience the upward-striving tree within them —

that is, the strength was not yet present in human beings to develop autonomously towards their divine, original home — pre-Christian initiates knew, nevertheless, that the time for this would eventually come. The Menorah, the upward-striving tree, is an embodiment of their Messiah expectation.

These words were living spiritual beings, and without melodic intonation they stood before the disciples in a previously unknown reality, joined to one another through particular spiritual ties. Together composing the Sephiroth, these spiritual beings were linked by the 22 letters — like helping, extended hands which join people together. Through these spiritual connections the disciples were granted insight into mystery secrets of the human being and his place in the cosmic course of evolution.

Today, without knowing the ancient language of Aramaic, we can still gain access to what dawned on the disciples through this language. We pursue the path of awareness, which the disciples once followed by speaking the Lord's Prayer, when we ascend the 'trunk' of the spiritual tree from the earthly realm up to heights of spirit — as the disciples did after their initiating vision of the 'tree', and when, as symbol of this insight and knowledge, they added the words of the doxology to the prayer of the Logos, to affirm and strengthen it.

Study of the spiritual secrets underlying the paths designated by Hebrew letters leads us to a first sense of the wealth of spiritual wisdom contained in the mantric words of the prayer given by the Son of God.

The Path of Knowledge Through the Trunk of the Sephiroth Tree

Let us take the central axis, the trunk of the Sephiroth tree (see *Drawing 6*) to help visualize what is involved. From below — from earthly depths — we ascend alongside the disciples and now experience what was vouchsafed to them on this path through the language of their time:

ת 'TAW'

The first step which the Christian initiation pupil takes is that between the numbers 10 and 9 in an upward direction. The link between the numbers 10 and 9 is designated by the letter (ת) TAW, the last letter of the Hebrew alphabet. The sephira 10, *Malchut,* is the 'kingdom'. From the disciples' perspective, or from our own, we can say that this is the kingdom of God on earth, the earthly kingdom. The sephira 9, *Jesod,* is the 'power' or the 'foundation'. Simplifying, we can say that in 10 (the earthly kingdom) the human being lives in his waking consciousness, whereas in 9 he attains a different state of consciousness that is embodied in the symbol of the moon. During sleep the human being prepares to enter the world of spirit. In connection with the concluding words of the Lord's Prayer we saw that the human being approaches the Holy Spirit when he leaves matter behind and begins to perceive beyond its threshold. The TAW is the path of Parsifal or of Siegfried the dragon-slayer. In an ascending direction the human being must slay the dragon of maya or matter — he must pass the animals as he passes the Guardian of the Threshold. This is why the letter TAW bears the highest numerical value, 400, which ancient Hebrew tradition regarded as the greatest density of the physical world, and the most painful distance from the world of spirit. (In the Old Testament, for instance, we find the 400 years of the Israelites' enslavement in Egypt as expression of this distance.) On his path of evolution through the earthly world, the human being must first have arrived at the very deepest point, that is, have plumbed the densest degree of matter and become a fully earthly human being, before he can begin to develop out of himself the capacity to evolve towards spiritual ascent. Christ also accomplished His 'descent into hell', into the depths of *Malchut*, the earthly kingdom, in order to be able to recreate the human being's physical archetype. The God had to become mortal — that is, follow the path of TAW downwards (from 9 to 10) — in order to rise into the earthly kingdom, from where He rose further again into the etheric world. Thus we follow the Christ by pursuing the TAW path from 10 to 9.

ס 'SSAMECH'

The link between 9, *Jesod,* and 6, *Tiphereth,* represents the transition to a still more elevated state of awareness, and is expressed by the essence of the letter ס SSAMECH. This links the symbols of sun and moon. *Tiphereth* is the sun, the harmony of the Son, which balances the whole tree in a kind of Michaelic scales. Thus SSAMECH links dream consciousness or incipient spiritual vision with Christian initiate consciousness. One could also invoke representatives of human evolution or the elements in order to distinguish between *Jesod* and *Tiphereth.* The relationship between them is like that between Moses and Elijah, or moon and sun, water and air, female and male, or between Joachim and Boaz.

The letter SSAMECH, as the being characteristic of the path between the two Sephiroths, also however draws our attention to the danger into which the initiation pupil can fall if he turns to Lucifer instead of striving towards Christ. SSAMECH is an old word for 'snake', from which the word for poison (SSAM) is derived. Remarkably the newer Hebrew word 'snake' and the word 'Messiah' have the same numerical value (if one adds the numerical values of the letters together): that is, 358. In the Hebraic view of numbers this is anything other than coincidental.

On the path to Christ the human being can succumb to the snake, for the activity of the snake in the world of spirit is still more dazzling than in the earthly world. We need to know this in order to arm and defend ourselves.

ג 'GIMEL'

The link with the essence of the letter (ג) GIMEL — which bears the numerical value 3 — breaks through the boundary between the earthly quadrilateral and the divine triangle, and leads to the tree's crown, the highest of all human paths of evolution.

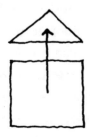

Drawing 7

In Aramaic, GIMEL is really GAMEL and means 'camel'. We know the parable that corresponds with this. The disciples could of course understand Jesus' parables much better than we can. The metaphor of the camel that passes through the eye of a needle did not surprise them. Needle's eye in Aramaic is 'KOF', the name for the letter with the numerical value 100. In other words the GIMEL, 3, has to pass through the KOF, 100 — a true image for the fact that all three lower bodily sheaths must be worked upon by the 'I' in order to attain to the *One,* the crown of spiritual evolution. (The two zeros after the 1 represent stages of evolving consciousness, the path into the world of spirit through *Jesod* and *Tiphereth*.) This is why the Bible also says: No one comes to the Father except through me! The human being has to pass *through* the sephira *Tiphereth,* the Son of God, in order to reach God the Father.

I wanted to give this summation of the wealth of knowledge revealed to the disciples and the women by Jesus Christ Himself, in full earthly embodiment, when He spoke these words to them.

The Lord's Prayer Grows as Human Beings Evolve

The very special quality of this prayer, given to us directly from the mouth of Christ, is that it grows with us as we evolve. The further humanity develops its spirit consciousness, the more will the depths of these words be revealed. In early Christianity the Lord's Prayer was still fully one with the God who proclaimed it. It was simply referred to and inwardly absorbed as 'The Word of the Lord'. During the Middle Ages, when faith gave people support and strength, it continually accompanied them through their lives. Continually praying it strengthened the etheric body in particular. Today and in the future, as we acquire the consciousness soul, the Lord's Prayer will gain ever more of an apocalyptic dimension for human beings: we will come to recognize how profound these apparently simple words actually are, and what they contain and can activate for our spiritual path of evolution.

Ever new things about the spiritual world will be revealed to us through this prayer, in every future age. The everlasting constant, however, which never leaves us, whatever incarnation we are in — a fact that is anchored in the solace of these words — is that the moment we speak the prayer in true and honest fashion, we find ourselves as though safely mantled by the Godhead, wrapped in a spiritual space of protection against all powers of darkness.

Thus the disciples experienced, as do we too, the passage of the Word through earthly embodiment as it unites in a Holy Trinity with human evolution:

'In the beginning was the Word'

the Word

(at **stage 1** of human evolution)

↓

*'And the Word became flesh
and dwelt among us'*

↓

the Word
(at **stage 2** of human evolution)

*And it shall resound until it becomes as enlivened
through the human being himself as it once was
through the Logos*

the Word
(at **stage 3** of human evolution)

Personal Concluding Remarks

The content of this volume was originally presented in a lecture — that is, verbally. At the end of each of my talks I spoke the Lord's Prayer in the original Aramaic version, as it was spoken at the turning point of time and laid into human hearts by the Redeemer. Thus I was also willing to print the Aramaic Lord's prayer here, to conclude the transcript of the lecture content. In certain respects it represents the core of everything I have to say.

But when I arrived at this final page and tried to convert the sounds of the Aramaic words into something decipherable, I realized, after all, that this would be tantamount to violating the living quality of these sacred words.

Of course I am aware that this prayer has been translated into every language in the world and fixed in writing. There are even various Hebrew and

Aramaic versions,* none of which, however, as far as my comparative studies suggest, come close to the words actually spoken. One can conclude therefore that this form of new Aramaic at the time of Christ was not preserved — at least not as far as the original version of the Lord's Prayer is concerned.

And it seems to me that my sense of being unable to print the ancient Word is based on this. It would be well-nigh impossible to constrict these words in printed form, to press them into mechanical service as it were.

Day after day I have tried to grasp this intractable difficulty. I kept trying to integrate the phonic script of the words into this text, for I did not wish to lay myself and the volume open to the charge of lack of scholarly rigour.

However it is a palpable fact that the words, as the disciples heard them at the time, have not been preserved. This is astonishing when one considers

---

* These are almost always reconstructions from modern or past times, or transcripts from later centuries, which are nevertheless attributed to the early Christian period. (Author's note.)

that this is the best-known prayer in Christianity. But does it have to be chance, or a typical slow dilution of historical events? I believe that there is another reason, since the Lord's Prayer was not forgotten for a certain time and then later revived. On the contrary, it was first spoken by the original Christians, the disciples, after the Whitsun event, and thus passed on to those around them. As we know, the Whitsun event marked the moment when the disciples went out into the world to spread the Word of Christ through their own mouths and through their very personal connection to the Christ being. They did so with a certain degree of inexperience, yet nevertheless with a new self-awareness that had just been born in them. The Whitsun event gave them a new, hitherto unknown independence and self-reliance, and it was this experience especially which filled them with a new awareness of the words of Christ, the Lord's Prayer. They now recalled with keen clarity that they had been entrusted with the task of passing it on to the rest of humanity. Direct experience of the events at the turning point of time also confirms that some of the disciples and followers of Jesus Christ spoke this prayer shortly before the death they suffered for His sake.

We can therefore be sure that from the very beginning the Lord's Prayer was accorded great importance in the community of the early Christians. It was not forgotten. That the original Aramaic words of the prayer nevertheless did not survive is due, according to my findings, to the fact I have already stressed: that the living quality of these sacred words could only arise at all through the intimate *vernacular* of each speaker or listener. Just as every divine prayer, each true mantram, forms an intimate connection with the spirit of a language, so the spiritual reality of these words could only unfold where a person, adopting a corresponding stance of soul, entered into a sacred relationship with the Word, as his mother tongue rendered it comprehensible.

Only a few years after the death of Jesus, the prime field of activity of the early Christians shifted from Palestine to the Near East and to Rome — that is, into the areas where Greek and Latin were spoken. The Whitsun spirit enabled the early

Christians to adapt quickly to the different cultures and languages of the people living there, to whom they wished to bring the Word of Christ. And it is surely thanks to this Whitsun fire that, from being a tiny community, Christianity spread and grew so astonishingly quickly, for the words of those who proclaimed it united with the spirit of each nation and language with which they came into contact.

With the death of these original Judaic Christians, or at least no later than the death of their direct pupils, the Aramaic words spoken by Jesus Christ disappeared. But this was not in the least to be regretted. On the one hand these words had already performed their original service, enabling the early Christians who heard them to unite fully through their mother tongue with the prayer's being, essence and spiritual treasures. On the other hand, the natural confluence of Christ's Word with the spirits of the languages of other peoples — indeed, of all the peoples of the world — was firm proof of the swift path and welcoming reception that the Christ impetus took on its further journey beyond Palestine.

If, today, we once more have the capacity to encounter the original words and sounds of the Lord's Prayer through direct experience of the events at the time of Christ — words which are inscribed in the great book of human history and evolution — we awaken this original prayer of Jesus Christ to life again. Rudolf Steiner is right to describe this prayer as 'magical', for it was enlivened by Christ Himself.

This can only happen from mouth to ear. We have to *receive* it: then it makes its way from heart to heart, from spirit to spirit.

Yet where is the magical vitality of the world of spirit if the Word loses its breath and is constrained and truncated by being squeezed into print? Who, ultimately, would gain anything real from words that cannot, as originally, be spoken and absorbed personally and individually, but only generalized in print and thus killed? Even if the spoken Word appears to fade and dissipate, it remains within us forever since the soul and spirit has been able to undergo a true experience, to touch the hem of the divine world.

I therefore ask my readers to understand why I did not wish to print this living Word of God. I am however more than willing to speak these sacred words to anyone who requests this, as far as it lies in my capacity to render them truly.

And If He Has Not Been Raised...
The Stations of Christ's Path to Spirit Man
Judith von Halle

At Passiontide 2004, Judith von Halle received the stigmata — the duplication on her body of the wounds of Christ. Following a period of careful consideration, she eventually decided to share this intimate occurrence with a small group in Berlin in Michaelmas of that year. The phenomenon of the stigmata is usually either seen as a sheer miracle or is simply denied. In contrast, in her first lectures here, she attempts to arrive at a clear *understanding* of it — based on the spiritual scientific knowledge of Rudolf Steiner — and its significance for one's personal destiny.

As a consequence of receiving the stigmata, von Halle began to experience the events of the life of Christ in full, sensory detail. In addition, she has explored these events by means of spiritual-scientific research methods — sometimes referred to as 'continuity of consciousness'. In the further five lectures of this volume she offers a commentary to the Mystery of Golgotha, the turning-point in world history. Her intention is to stimulate the reader to reflect patiently and repeatedly upon this great Mystery, and to enter into an ever closer relationship to Christ.

Chapters:
— About the knowledge and reality of the Resurrection of Christ
— The significance of the phantom, the Resurrection Body, for an understanding of the human being
— The Mystery of Golgotha as the end of the old and beginning of the new initiation
— An account of the events between Death and Resurrection (Descent into Hell)
— The Transfiguration on Mount Tabor and the last night on the Mount of Olives
— The event of Easter at the time of Christ
— The event of Whitsun at the time of Christ and its connection with Anthroposophy

2007; 234 × 156 mm; paperback; £14.95;
ISBN 978 1902636 88 7